This Book Belongs To Ruth

With love & best wishes
from
Pam - Christmas 1991

By arrangement with the C. R. Gibson Co.,
this edition first published 1990 by
Dean, an imprint of The Octopus Publishing Group Limited
Michelin House, 81 Fulham Road, London SW3 6RB
Reprinted 1990

ISBN 0 600 57146 7

Printed in Hong Kong by Mandarin Offset.

An ALICE IN BIBLELAND® Storybook

The STORY Of JESUS And HIS DISCIPLES

Written by Alice Joyce Davidson
Designed by Victoria Marshall

Dean

A little girl named Alice
Likes to read her books a lot.
A bench right by her window
Is her favourite reading spot.

Whenever she's not busy
And she has an extra minute,
She reads her Bible storybook
And looks at pictures in it.

One day she read of Jesus,
How He looked until He found
Twelve friends, He called disciples,
To help spread God's Word around.

As Alice read, the airmail bird
Flew to her window sill
And dropped this special message
Which he carried in his bill:

"Reading is the magic key
To take you where you want to be."

Her book became a great big screen,
The screen grew tall and wide,
Then Alice took a little walk
To Bibleland inside.

She saw Jesus walking,
And much to her surprise
The story she was reading
Came to life before her eyes.

“The time is right,” thought Jesus,
“To go across the land
And tell the people whom I meet
God’s Kingdom’s close at hand.

"I want to teach and preach and help
Everyone I can,
But I will need disciples
To carry out this plan."

That day as He was strolling,
By the sea of Galilee,
He saw two brothers fishing,
Casting nets into the sea.

Andrew was one brother's name.
Peter was the other.
They both seemed good and honest,
And worked well with one another.

Jesus felt that He could trust
Brothers like these two,
So He called out to both of them
Across the sea of blue . . .

"Come with Me. You'll never have
To fish for fish again.
Follow Me and you'll become
My fishermen of men."

The brothers were quite puzzled,
Then each man on his own
Looked up at Jesus and saw
That love and goodness shone.

They came to shore to join Him.
And follow Jesus' way.
And they met two other brothers
Later on that day.

James and John were mending nets.
Their boat was on the shore.
Jesus said, "Here's two more men,
The kind I'm looking for.

"Come with Me. You'll never have
To fish for fish again.
Follow Me and you will be
My fishermen of men."

James and John looked at His face
And saw such goodness there,
They decided that they'd go with Him,
And follow everywhere.

Jesus told His four new friends
The news He wanted spread—
The good news that God's Kingdom
Is coming just ahead.

The four agreed, "We'll follow You
And be there when You preach,
And if You will instruct us,
We will help You teach."

Jesus was very happy
With the four new friends He found;
But He needed twelve disciples
To help spread the Word around.

So He made friends with Philip,
And with Bartholomew,
And a tax collector, Matthew,
Joined the others, too.

They met a man named Thomas,
Then found Thaddeus one day.
Both of them loved Jesus
So they followed in His way.

Then came a man whose name was James,
And faithful Simon, too,
Judas joined the others and
All said, "We'll follow You!"

Now Jesus had twelve special friends
And every one of them
Shared His news, and they became
Fishermen of men.

Everywhere they preached God's Word,
Great crowds would follow, too,
And every time that Jesus spoke,
The crowds just grew and grew.

Jesus spoke in simple language
That all could understand.
And His twelve friends helped spread His news
All across the land.

The time had come for Alice
To leave that Bible scene.
She thought of Jesus and His disciples
As she walked through her screen.

“How good it must have been to be
With Jesus every day,
To be His friend, and spread His word
And follow in His way.

"I'm glad that Jesus is my friend.
He's with me everywhere."
Then Alice put her book away
And knelt and said this prayer:

"Dear Jesus, You're my closest Friend.
You teach me and You guide me.
It feels so good each day to know
That You are here beside me.

"Thank You for Your loving words,
Your kind forgiving ways,
I will be Your disciple
And follow You all my days!"